CONSCIOUS PERSONAL PRODUCTIVITY IN ONE WEEK

HOW TO BE MORE PRODUCTIVE, STOP PROCRASTINATING, LEARN HOW TO FREE YOURSELF FROM STRESS, WAYS TO INCREASE WORK EFFICIENCY

Jorge O. Chiesa

Copyright 2019© Jorge O. Chiesa

All rights reserved. No part of this publication may be reproduced or distributed in any form or by any means, electronic or mechanical, including photocopying, recording, or by any information storage or retrieval system, without the prior written permission of the authors.

   First Edition

Índex

Introduction: Create your own game plan! 5
Learn how to reduce distractions 9
What's the first thing I have to do? 13
    You must exercise your self-discipline 16
    You're capable of doing the impossible. 19
Increase your motivation to its maximum potential
.... 22
    Don't let unpleasant moments make you give
    in! 25
    Always keep in mind your goals 28
Take care of yourself! 31
Why is organization so important in your life? 34
    Delegation: the main ingredient of productivity
.... 37
How do I avoid being exhausted by being
productive? 40
Always have provisions 43
    The importance of a positive state of mind 46

Do not fall in the face of evil... Also known as negativity 49

   Complete the tasks of your objective..... Or you won't get anything 52

   Let's talk about collaborators and employees 55

Pleasing yourself... It's the best thing you can do ...58

Don't give power to work overload 61

   The real reason why you should relax more often...64

   Set your priorities like a king................................67

   Maximize your communication skills.................70

Conclusion: The cornerstone of all success... The strategies! 73

Introduction: Create your own game plan!

One factor that all successful people have in common is effective time management. You may prefer to call it structure, get the job done, or a game plan. Any word or term that works for you is fine. As long as you take it seriously and put it into practice, you'll be creating one of the basic principles of productivity.

It might be a good idea to think about this, and why this factor is so essential to success. Maybe you can start by thinking the opposite: ways that don't work. Even if you have a very small task to complete, if you don't manage your time properly, it may be done too late, or not done at all. You may be working on a deadline, or have a task that does not have a specific time to be completed. If you do not have a game plan to do so, the results will not be satisfactory. While procrastination and wasted time prevent productivity, the lack of effective time management can be so destructive.

Increasing your productivity and getting things done means having a good game plan. First, you need to know exactly what needs to be done. Second, even if you don't have a specific deadline, you must also decide when to do it. The third step is to get to the task of doing it.

You want to achieve your goals, whether they are short-term or long-term. You also want to be proud and satisfied with the results. When you're not content with just "going with the flow," and instead take your game plan seriously every step of the way, you're almost guaranteed success, pride, and satisfaction.

Structure and time management can be easy for you, if they have been a regular part of your life. If you are not used to these concepts, now is the time to implement them in your daily life. Whether you are setting up your own business, working for someone else, or if your job is to take care of your family, you will reap many benefits from establishing a good game plan.

If you've ever felt that there aren't enough hours in a day to do everything you need to do, this will be a very positive step for you. You will be pleasantly surprised with everything you can accomplish. With a game plan, you can find yourself doing more every day than you normally do in a week. Not only will you be more productive, but achieving each goal will be much easier. You will soon appreciate this important factor in your success.

Learn how to reduce distractions

There are few things that block productivity as quickly as distractions do. When you can't concentrate and focus correctly, you can't do things. Even if you accomplish something, it can feel stressful and frustrating. Whether at work or school, reducing distractions that influence your ability to be productive will help you do more.

There are two key points to keep in mind when planning to reduce distractions in your environment. The first point is what works for you and what works for someone else may be completely different. The second point is that unless you have examined your habits, you may not be 100% sure which ones are most effective for you. The good news is that it doesn't take much time or effort to consider how your habits are affecting your productivity, and start adjusting them accordingly.

If you're like most people these days, multitasking has become a part of your daily life and vocabulary. There may be a number of things you need to do in a day, and you may be doing them simultaneously. If you exceed yourself with multitasking, there can be two consequences. It is possible that not everything will be done, or that it will disperse too much and not have satisfactory results.

The same can be said of distractions. Trying to do a job, and doing it correctly and well, will not give satisfactory results if distractions are allowed to get in the way. Working while listening to music, watching TV or talking on the phone is not limited to teenagers. Many adults do these things in their home office, and even in an office that is occupied by others. They may help you concentrate, but they can also ruin your concentration and distract you from what you're doing. Becoming more productive requires a little analysis of your habits. You can turn off some or all of these distractions and see if you can concentrate better on the task at hand. You may find that you can do the job better, faster, and more effectively, without any distractions at all. On the other hand, you may find that one of these factors really helps your concentration and focus.

While finding what works for you is easy if you work on your own, it can be a bit more complicated if you work with others. You may find that co-workers who constantly use their phones, visit or play their radios near your workplace distract you from concentrating on your work. If you approach them politely, this may be all it takes to reduce distractions so you can concentrate on your work.

What's the first thing I have to do?

If you think back to when you were in school, you may remember that teachers told you that the best way to approach homework and other projects was to do the hardest homework first. You may also have been advised to address the topic of the homework you disliked the most before moving on. This same approach can greatly improve your productivity today.

When you are preparing to start a new day's work, try to start putting this approach into practice. Instead of starting with a task you like or find easy, start with one you don't like or find very difficult. At the end of the day, you may be pleasantly surprised at how much you have accomplished. You will also feel that the day has gone much smoother.

One reason is that at the beginning of your workday you will have more energy. When you devote this energy to the most difficult or distasteful tasks, you won't feel so exhausted or frustrated doing them. A second reason is that if you start with tasks you enjoy, you often find yourself looking forward to those you don't like in a very negative way. Instead of enjoying the easier tasks as you do them, fear the ones that await you. When you do the harder ones first, not only will you have more energy left for the rest of the day, but you'll also appreciate the other tasks more when you get there.

This approach will increase your productivity. When you don't see your workday as a long, uphill battle, you'll have more accomplishments. Eliminating unpleasant tasks first, early in the day, will generate better results with all your tasks. Not only will you do more, but you will be much more satisfied with the outcome of each and every task.

While it is only human nature to want to do what you like first, having the most difficult things on the horizon can slow you down and drain your energy. If you want to be more productive and achieve the best results in everything you do, follow the advice of your school teachers and do the hardest work first. Your productivity will increase, and you'll end each day with a refreshing sense of accomplishment.

You must exercise your self-discipline

Self-discipline is an essential factor for productivity and success. Without it, one becomes lazy, unmotivated and dependent on others. Lack of self-discipline also makes it difficult to deal with an employee, boss, or co-worker.

Exercising self-discipline means, in an old-fashioned term, getting down to a task. You need to know what to do, when to do it, and do it. Good self-discipline includes a basic schedule, or framework, of what needs to be accomplished within a specific period of time. You don't allow yourself to stray, or leave things for later.

However, being too rigid with self-discipline does not increase productivity. It may even diminish it. If no rest is allowed throughout the working day, or no margin for error at all, the expectations you are imposing on yourself are too rigid. Instead of doing more things, or doing more in less time, you can make him frustrated with his tasks and his work.

If you learned self-discipline at an early age, you probably won't have any difficulty with it now. On the other hand, if your years of schooling and family life were too rigid, or if little was expected of you, this is a good time to develop the habit. You may have managed to slip through your early years without a good sense of self-discipline, but it will be a stumbling block for your career.

A good way to start cultivating self-discipline is to recognize what you are responsible for. You can start by taking responsibility for getting the job done right and on time. If this is a relatively new concept to you, you also need to recognize that mistakes occur, and be able to correct them without undue frustration.

Exercising self-discipline also includes not being led astray by distractions and time-wasting activities. While you may need and deserve a little rest during your workday, this cannot divert you from the route of doing the work. Once you have developed the habit of self-discipline, it will be easier to complete tasks. They will be done well, and on time. It will increase your productivity and help you get closer to success.

You're capable of doing the impossible.

If you've ever had so many different tasks to complete, or tasks that seemed beyond your capabilities, you know what it's like to feel impossible. When these kinds of tasks are within your scope of responsibility, there are some positive ways to approach them. You may find that you can really do the impossible.

Sometimes you may see tasks as impossible because you are overwhelmed by how much you need to do in a short period of time. Even if each of them is pretty simple, it can become a mountain of work that you can't reasonably expect to be finished. This can happen when you take more than you can handle, or when unexpected "surprises" arise without proper preparation.

A positive approach to the above situation is to be reasonable about what you can do at first. Whether taking on too many responsibilities is due to a financial need, trying to look good for your boss or outdo a co-worker, or not thinking about it when you take on each task, assessing your capabilities beforehand can eliminate this problem. A positive approach to the latter situation is to learn how to set priorities. If an unexpected task or project arises while you are dealing with your other tasks, you must decide which tasks should be completed immediately and which can wait until later. In many cases, asking for more time to do everything is a good idea.

Sometimes you may have a project that is really beyond your capabilities. In these cases, the best approach is to recognize its limitations. Depending on the circumstances, you may ask for help or state that you cannot.

Good time management and clear recognition of your skills are the keys to doing the impossible. Instead of being overwhelmed by work, or stressed by something you are simply unable to do, you will be increasing your energy and self-esteem. While no one can do everything, and no one can do everything equally well, you will be doing the best you can. This, in turn, will reduce the feeling of being overwhelmed and help you be much more productive.

Increase your motivation to its maximum potential

We've all heard people say "they weren't motivated" as an excuse not to do things. In most cases, this is a polite way of saying they are lazy. In the real world, where productivity and success are essential, motivation is a key element. If it's not natural for you, you can examine ways to increase your own motivation and put it into practice every day.

The more motivated you are, the more you can do. One way you can try to increase your motivation is to enjoy and appreciate your accomplishments. Instead of waiting until you have reached your goal, start by enjoying and appreciating every task you perform along the way. While you shouldn't waste time or stray from the path, patting yourself figuratively on the back for well-completed and correctly completed tasks can be a great way to increase your motivation. You will want to do more; and you will want to continue to excel.

By doing this, you will also help increase your stamina. Instead of feeling overwhelmed by a main objective on the horizon, which can leave you tired and stressed, you can make you feel more energetic and better prepared for the next task.

It is easy for a person to lose their sense of motivation when they feel they are not achieving anything. This can make you not feel very good about what you are doing, or even do less. Fortunately, it's not hard to reverse this pattern and get ahead. When you get used to being happy with every task you do, and take pride in each and every accomplishment, it will increase your motivation to do even more, and to do better each time.

   As motivation and energy are connected, you will also see that you have much more energy for all the tasks ahead of you. No matter how big your ultimate goal is, or how much time and work you need to devote to it to achieve that particular goal, you will be pleasantly surprised at how well everything progresses. As your motivation and energy increase, you will be able to do more and more. You'll see how great productivity can be every day.

Don't let unpleasant moments make you give in!

One of the biggest obstacles to productivity is the approach many people take to overcome setbacks. If you see a setback as a failure, you may not only limit your productivity, but you may prevent you from doing anything at all. This is true in any line of work, schooling, or any other area of life. When you see a setback as a failure, you can stop it from moving forward. You may accomplish less, or you may accomplish nothing at all.

Setbacks occur in all areas of life. No matter what kind of work you have, you are likely to experience it from time to time or on a regular basis. Setbacks can occur from making mistakes, being unprepared for what you need to do, or unexpected problems that aren't anyone's fault. The way you experience and see a setback determines how it will affect you and your productivity.

However, there is a perspective that can prevent you from becoming an obstacle and, in fact, increase your productivity. If the setback was due to a mistake on your part, or if it wasn't anyone's fault, refusing to see it as a failure is the first step to getting you back on track.

The second step is to see the reverse as an opportunity to do better next time. If you have made a mistake in your work, the best approach is to try to correct the mistake and move on. While it is essential that you don't try to cover up a mistake, you can't afford to let a mistake stop you. If you don't correct it and move on, you may find yourself thinking about it. You may punish yourself for the mistake, or even obsess over it. These behaviors are never helpful. Not only will they keep you from doing things, but they will also make you feel bad about yourself. In the worst case, it can make you feel incompetent. This is not the way to do things.

Seeing each setback as a learning experience is a much better approach. You can tell yourself that you are capable of doing better, and capable of doing more. As long as they look at the setbacks this way, rather than as failures, they won't stop them from moving forward. Correct the mistake and learn from it, and move on. When you have developed this pattern, and make it a regular part of your working life, setbacks will not stand in the way of being productive.

Always keep in mind your goals

"If you don't know where you're going, you may never reach your destination." New York Yankees player and coach Yogi Berra was on target when he made that statement. It's an excellent thought to keep in mind for your work life.

You may be surprised at how many people don't know what they're looking for in their work life. On the other hand, you could be one of those people. If so, now is the time to focus on your goals. When you know where you're going, that's one of the most important steps to make sure you get there.

When you prepare to go to work in the morning, what's the first thought that crosses your mind about the subject of your goal? If you are like many people, you do not think of it in terms of a goal at all. Instead, you may be thinking about how much work you will have to do, or how good the paycheck will be at the end of the week. If you change your thoughts to a goal, you'll be much more productive.

Depending on the nature of your work, goals can take a variety of different forms. You may have something to produce on your own, or you may be part of a team. You may have a very positive sense of self-discipline, or work very well as a team player. Whatever your place in your work life, being goal-oriented will increase your productivity.

Being goal-oriented doesn't have to mean focusing on just one big achievement. If you start looking at it as a number of small goals, each one you reach will give you two benefits. Each of them will motivate you more to continue, as well as to get closer to the great achievement.

Nothing can be achieved overnight. All that is really worthwhile requires time, effort and work. When you set your sights on the big goal in the distance, and on each of the goals you need to achieve to get there, you will soon see how much more productive you will be at each step of the way. Simply going with the flow and not putting your emphasis on your goals will slow you down. You won't accomplish much if you don't focus on achievement. When you know where you're going, it's the safest way to know you'll get there.

Take care of yourself!

If you're like most people, you've probably had the experience of working all night to do something. You may not have slept, missed meals, and other important self-care factors in order to complete a task or meet a deadline. Although it is sometimes necessary to do this, neglecting self-care on a regular or frequent basis will be counterproductive. Your health may suffer as long as you are not achieving almost everything you expected.

Taking care of yourself will not only keep you in good health, but also keep you productive. A person who does not sleep regularly, or who relies on junk food instead of eating nutritious food, will not be physically or mentally up to the task.

While you may believe that you are giving one hundred percent to your work, these unhealthy habits result in having less to give.

On the other hand, if you get enough sleep on a regular basis and make sure you have a healthy diet, you will have more to give to your job. When you are in a first-class condition, you will concentrate better, be more alert, and not fatigue as easily. You'll do better, and you'll do more.

If your workday has consisted of drinking plenty of coffee or other artificial energy stimulants, it's time to examine your self-care habits. If you find that you haven't been getting enough sleep and have been relying on these products to keep you functioning, or if you find that good nutrition has been replaced by junk food and snacks, it's time to evaluate what these habits are doing to your overall health. It's also time to think about the effects you may be having on your job.

   Although almost everyone is occasionally in a position to skip a meal or work late at night, if these have become habits for you, it is unlikely that they are helping you to be more productive. In fact, they're probably holding you back.

   Even if you have a fast-paced job with many responsibilities and deadlines, neglecting proper self-care is counterproductive. When you begin to develop the habit of getting enough sleep and eating a proper diet, you will be doing more than taking care of yourself. You'll get more done, and you'll be more satisfied with the results.

Why is organization so important in your life?

If you think about it, being organized is one of the most essential factors for being productive. You don't need to be extremely rigid to be organized, but you do need to be aware of everything that happens in your workday. Doing things means being organized with your time, the supplies and equipment you use, and your expectations.

You may think of someone who is disorganized, and how it affects their work. You may rush into the workday, miss appointments, be unsure of what to accomplish, and be careless with the supplies or equipment you work with during the day. This is a person who doesn't get things done, because being disorganized prevents him from being productive.

You will get a lot more in a shorter period of time if you are well organized. You can start by making a basic schedule of what you need to do and when you should do it. You can make sure you know in advance where all your supplies are, so you don't waste time looking for something when you need to use it.

Being organized with time elements and materials is not difficult at all. However, if you haven't yet cultivated this habit, it may require a little practice before it begins to feel completely natural to you. Preparing an outline of your work day will help you be where you need to be, and get things done on time. Keeping all your supplies tidy and organized will help you avoid wasting time and getting frustrated that you can't easily find items when you need them.

When your goal is to increase your productivity - to get things done - being organized is an essential factor. If you are one of the many people who have not yet developed this positive habit, the results may surprise you. You'll soon see that you're accomplishing a lot more, doing a better job and ending up with more satisfying results. Being better organized in all aspects of your work life will greatly improve your productivity.

Delegation: the main ingredient of productivity

There are two different types of delegation that are both negative. Both can inhibit rather than increase productivity. If you recognize any of these factors in your work life, you can begin to change them for better results.

The first negative form of delegating involves the person who wants to do everything for themselves. While this may look positive at first, it's not really positive at all. The person who insists on taking on more work than he or she can reasonably do, or work that he or she is not fully capable of doing on his or her own, not only becomes less productive, but also affects the productivity of everyone who relies on him or her to do the work. Whether he is afraid to ask for help, or simply boasts, this can slow everyone else down, as well as himself.

The second negative way of delegating involves the person who shirks his or her own responsibilities. He can ask others to do tasks that he really should be doing himself. Not only is he not carrying his own weight, but he is occupying other people's valuable time.

Positive delegation is sensible. When you recognize that you can't do everything, and that you can't do everything equally well, you're increasing your own productivity as well as the productivity of those around you.

When you have a very large or very difficult task or project, ask others to help you get the job done, and do it faster.

Instead of considering delegation as an admission of weakness or incompetence, you are recognizing the scope of your own role and your own capabilities. This, in turn, will give others the opportunity to collaborate and help get the job done.

Delegating for doing less than you can do, or less than you can reasonably be expected to do, is always negative. However, when faced with more work than you can reasonably do on your own, or work that you are not able to do on your own, delegation is the sensible solution. When a job needs to be done, and on time, and well, teamwork will give the best results.

How do I avoid being exhausted by being productive?

There is very little that can cause a decrease in productivity as easily as burnout. While you may be tempted to believe that putting every moment of your life to work on your job is a good way to do things, there is an additional factor that you may not have considered. When you take your work home figuratively, you can increase the risk of burnout and accomplish much less in the long run.

This way of taking your work home does not involve doing some essential work during your free time. It involves keeping your work in your mind during your free time. When you're at home, or anywhere other than your workplace, you can easily get burned if you keep it as your main objective.

During your free time, you can spend a lot of time thinking about your work. You can worry about whether you are going to do something on time, or about the overall quality of your work. This can lead you to be too stressed, anxious and overwhelmed. You may feel more fatigued by your work when you're thinking about it and worrying about it than when you're actually doing your job.

If you don't have work to complete after your normal workday, you can avoid burnout by leaving your work at your workplace when you go home. Instead of stressing out about what you need to accomplish the next day, or about the progress you're making with something you're working on, try to learn to leave those thoughts and worries at your workplace.

When you have free time, develop some positive habits. Learning to relax, participate in healthy recreational activities, and devote your time and concentration to friends and family will reduce the risk of burnout. Once you've begun to develop these habits, it won't be long before you see the results. You will start each new work day feeling physically, emotionally, and mentally refreshed. You will have more to give to your work when it cools down. You will be more motivated, more energetic and more productive.

Always have provisions

You may have heard the old saying that a good worker always takes care of his tools. This is equally relevant, whether you work in an office, in a workplace, or from home. Keeping all your supplies in excellent working condition and easily accessible will make you more productive.

No matter what type of supplies you use during your average workday, negligence can slow you down. You can't do effective work if your supplies are broken, damaged or worn from use. If you try to use supplies that are not in good condition, the quality of your work may be affected. It can take you much longer to do things, and they won't do as well as they would with supplies that are in perfect condition.

Think of it this way: if you're trying to work on a computer that's not up to scratch, or using a hand tool that's bent or damaged, or a piece of office equipment that stops while you're operating it, your productivity can come to a complete standstill. You may get frustrated or angry, and possibly not do the job at all.

When all your supplies, tools, and equipment are kept in ideal condition, they are better able to do the job properly. Your work won't slow down and you won't risk mistakes from faulty equipment. A good supply in good condition means doing things and having the best results.

No matter how quick you are to complete a task and finish a day's work, taking a few minutes to make sure everything is in good condition will save you time and eliminate unnecessary frustration. You can also make an effort to replace damaged supplies or equipment as soon as possible. You can take this new positive habit even further by making sure that all your supplies and equipment are kept where they belong when you're done using them.

These new habits will benefit you, as well as everyone who uses the same supplies and equipment. When everything is checked and stored in good condition, everyone will be in good condition and easily accessible the next time you or someone else needs them. This will make your workday much smoother, and you will be more productive.

The importance of a positive state of mind

Nothing has the power to increase your productivity as safely and easily as a positive mood. While you may not have the time or inclination to repeat statements to yourself throughout the workday, it is essential to recognize that your thinking influences and affects your productivity.

If you have problems in your personal life, the more you are able to keep them out of your workday, the better your performance will be. Even if something is especially problematic, you should do everything possible to keep your personal problems separate from your work life. If there is something you need help with, getting help during your free time can prevent it from interfering with your work.

On the other hand, if there is something negative in your work life, it should be addressed and dealt with as soon as possible. Feeling overwhelmed, anxious, stressed or overwhelmed will only slow you down.

The more you are able to remain positive and optimistic, the more you will achieve. Even if you face a task that is especially big or difficult, a positive mood can help you achieve more than you thought you could.

You can't do anything all at once. Sometimes it takes a lot of small steps to do something. Sometimes mistakes and setbacks occur. However, when you keep in mind that each step is bringing you closer to your goal, you are on the right track. When you tell yourself that every small accomplishment is a goal accomplished in itself, you are giving yourself the encouragement and motivation you need to succeed.

   Having a positive mood is not natural for everyone. If you are one of the many people who have never thought much about it, today is the ideal time to start. A positive mood will allow you to feel more confident in yourself and more confident in your abilities. Even if self-confidence is a relatively new experience for you, you'll be reaping the rewards in no time. You'll soon see how much a positive mood affects how much you do, and how happy you are with the results. You will be more productive and more satisfied with the outcome.

Do not fall in the face of evil... Also known as negativity

Negativity is a big obstacle to productivity. It also ensures that whatever is done is neither satisfactory nor appreciated. Whether the negativity you need to resist is yours or someone else's, the sooner it is resolved, the sooner you will be back on the right track.

Neglectivity can come in many forms, and all of them are counterproductive. Neglectivity can come in the form of contempt. You may not be sure of your ability to do the job or to do it well. If you believe that failure is on the horizon, this is the surest way to make it happen. You can resist the negativity of underestimation by reminding yourself of your competence. You may have to practice this regularly. When you do not allow a negative light to overshadow your abilities, this will prevent you from stopping.

Negative can also come in the form of a complaint. Whether you are complaining about your work or something else in your life, this kind of negativity can affect your work. Complaints wear you down and ruin your ability to concentrate properly. When you resist complaining every time you feel the desire to do so, you will be taking steps to keep negativity out of your work life. Instead of getting tired and grumpy about complaining, your energy level will be at its best.

Worry is another form of negativity. It can slow you down and make you less productive. While it may sound difficult, a good approach is to remind yourself that worrying accomplishes nothing. If the issue is something you can resolve, doing so as quickly as possible will reduce your concern. If it can't be dealt with immediately, try not to worry while working. You may even have to tell yourself that worrying about yourself won't solve a problem. This will help you concentrate better.

If you find that your negativity is extreme, asking for outside help may be helpful. You can learn to be in a better mood. This is better for your overall health, and also better for your productivity. The more you are able to resist negativity on a regular basis, the more you will achieve.

Complete the tasks of your objective..... Or you won't get anything

Some people have a habit of seeing their goal as the main thing they need to achieve. They may even consider it the only thing they need to accomplish. If this sounds like you, you're missing something very important that can increase your productivity. If you look at each and every task you need to complete to reach your goal as something very important in itself, your progress will be much smoother and you will be able to do more.

A good way to think about this is in terms of building a house. If you only think of the finished house, you are missing all the steps along the way. There are many steps necessary to build a house. None can be omitted or done wrong if you want the house to be strong and in excellent condition when finished.

The goals you have in your work life are similar. Regardless of what your particular goal is, there are a number of steps you must take to achieve it. To get the best possible results, each task along the way requires your time, effort, hard work and concentration.

If you have a very important goal ahead of you, you may be tempted to shorten some of the intermediate tasks. You may even have the idea that rushing through your tasks will help you reach the final goal much sooner. This is never a good approach. When you don't give your best on each and every task, no matter how small, the end results won't be as satisfying as you expect.

Giving your best to each task doesn't mean making something seem more important than it really is, wasting time or forgetting your ultimate goal. Giving your best means making sure that every task you do gets the time and attention it deserves. This means that even the smallest jobs are taken just as seriously as the biggest.

Devoting an appropriate amount of time and attention to each of the tasks you do will not delay you. In fact, it can help you be better motivated for each task ahead. When you give your best to everyone, no matter how small, you are increasing your chances of being fully satisfied with the end results when you reach your greatest goals.

Let's talk about collaborators and employees

There is a trend that is popular in the business world today. Some people believe that competition is the best way to boost productivity. No matter what line of work you're in, this approach is likely to be counterproductive.

First, teamwork is much better than competition. When you use the approach that everyone is working for the common good of the company, more will be done. When the sense of competition is eliminated, each person will want to bring out the best in themselves, simply because it is up to them to do so. You won't feel you have to outdo your co-workers, which in turn will increase the sense of teamwork. When everyone is working in a team, and working toward a common goal, productivity will increase.

Second, everyone needs to feel valued. This is just as true in the workplace as anywhere else. The best employee, and the one who does the most, is the one who believes their work is appreciated.

Another factor in increasing productivity is reducing the amount of stress, friction and conflict in the workplace. When there are employees who strive not to get along with others, expect someone else to do their job for them, or are simply difficult to be with them on a regular basis, these kinds of problems should be dealt with as quickly as possible. All that is needed is for one or two people who like to argue, or shirk their responsibilities to others, to turn any workplace into an uncomfortable place where no one can concentrate on doing their job. It is important to eliminate these problems so that everyone in the workplace can do things.

Productivity is highest in the workplace, where everyone present gets along well. This does not mean wasting time with unnecessary chats and visits. It is usually enough to recognize that everyone is there for the same purpose.

The workplace should be a place where every employee feels comfortable. It should be a place where everyone knows that all co-workers have the same goals in mind. When each person knows they are a valuable part of the company, and a valuable part of the team, each person will feel safer and be more productive.

Pleasing yourself... It's the best thing you can do

Encouraging yourself by rewarding yourself along the line can be a good thing. Unfortunately, if approached the wrong way, it can be more problematic than it's worth. If you think you owe yourself free time, special treats, or something more worth mentioning every time you accomplish something, you'll soon find yourself accomplishing very little. Instead of seeing it as a reward for a job well done, you may begin to feel that you have a right to receive rewards or special favors for completing tasks that are within your scope of responsibility anyway.

That's why it's not usually a good idea to give yourself small "extras" to do your job. It's even more negative if you expect special recognition or rewards from your boss or co-workers for doing what you're supposed to do. Rewarding yourself along the line as if you had done a spectacular achievement is not the best way to do the job.

Instead, applying some self-breath should be the only reward you need. When you complete a task on time, or do an especially good project, you may recognize that it is a small but important success. When you apply this type of self-stimulation with a figurative pat on the back, you are rewarding yourself for a job well done. You will also be prepared to move on to the next task or step.

This concept works equally well whether you work alone or in a group. If no one feels compelled to believe that they should get some kind of special recognition for doing their job, the priority will be to do it. In work environments that include a number of people working together as a group, no one will feel more or less important than others. Each person will realize that they are expected to contribute something, without expecting to receive anything unique for doing so.

   Encouraging yourself along the way will serve to keep your spirit high and your sense of motivation at its peak. While significant accomplishments may result in some kind of extra reward, self-breath should be the only reward necessary to do your job.

Don't give power to work overload

There are two ways you can overload yourself. You may take on more work than you are reasonably able to do; or you may take on work that is beyond your capabilities. Both can overload your energy, frustrate you, and discourage you. They also result in decreased productivity.

You may know someone who is a workaholic. You may be finding some aspect of your job to do long after you have left the workplace. You may feel that there is always something else you need to do, many hours after you leave work. This person may feel that no work will be done, or that it will not be done properly, unless he is doing it himself.

If you are this person, now is a good time to evaluate your overextended habits. While you surely want to be conscientious and complete everything that is your responsibility, overburdening yourself will not make you more productive. It can have exactly the opposite effect.

Stretching too much on a regular basis will wear you out, burn you out and wreak havoc on your health. Allowing yourself into this condition can affect your ability to concentrate and focus properly. You may start making unnecessary mistakes, or become forgetful. You won't get to do everything you expected.

You may resist overextending yourself by being reasonable about both your abilities and your time. Even if you're working on a very important project, you can't put "24/7" in it and hope it goes well. You need to take a reasonable amount of time to rest, eat and exercise, and even some recreation, in order to be in the best condition to do the job.

Going too far when trying to do work that is beyond your capabilities can also be counterproductive. If you're not fully qualified to do it, it won't work. Rather than overextend yourself with something you know you can't do, it's best to leave it to someone who is really qualified to complete it correctly.

You don't need to be discouraged about your work. If you try not to overextend yourself, you will be more productive than if you try to do everything yourself.

The real reason why you should relax more often

Stress has many results and none of them are positive. Stress results can hinder a job. Even if a job is finished, stress results can minimize your sense of accomplishment and satisfaction. When you become de-stressed, you will give the best of yourself and appreciate the result.

Since each person is an individual, it may be helpful for you to determine the best ways to de-stress. A coffee break, a brisk walk, or thinking about something completely different for a few minutes are some of the ways that may be helpful to you. Your own personality and individual needs should be the deciding factors. A method that works for one person doesn't necessarily work as well for the next.

If you don't destresasas when necessary, you won't do much. Stress can nullify your concentration, leaving you focused on everything other than the task at hand. Too much stress, especially if it's prolonged, can make you feel fatigued and physically ill. In addition to causing headaches and a general feeling of discomfort, prolonged stress even has the power to weaken your immune system. In the worst case scenario, extreme and prolonged stress can result in medical complications.

When stress has the power to cause all of these problems, it should be easy to see how it can affect your work. That's why de-stressing when necessary shouldn't be considered a luxury, a nonsense, or a waste of time. Neglecting the need for stress may prevent something from being done.

De-stress should not be seen as an excuse. Once you have begun to evaluate the effects of stress on your work life, it should not be difficult to determine when the need to de-stress arises. However, neither you nor your job can afford to use stress relief as an excuse to be lazy or irresponsible. With only a small amount of practice, realizing when stress is starting to have an effect on your job will be easy. A short break for any specific type of stress relief method is most appropriate for you to reduce or relieve your stress. When you don't feel overwhelmed by stress, it will be easier to concentrate on what you are doing and do it.

Set your priorities like a king

When you're at work, pretty much everything you do is important. However, setting and ranking your priorities will help you keep everything in the right perspective. This is a positive way of doing things.

Setting and ranking priorities means recognizing that some tasks require more time than others, and that some tasks require more work than others. If you make the mistake of trying to allocate the same amount of time to each task, it will delay you and not achieve as much as it should.

While you want to do your best on each task, determining which ones will require more time and effort is a much more productive approach than trying to see everything the same way.

Setting and ranking your priorities also means determining which tasks must be completed first. You can imagine that this is only logical, but often it doesn't happen that way. There may be a very large project on the horizon, which will require significantly more time and effort than the smaller projects you have on hand. Perhaps there is one that includes an important timeline, or even a deadline. In cases like these, you may have been tempted to make the tasks smaller and easier first. While this means that these easier tasks will be completed, it is possible that the one you should have paid attention to in the first place will not.

When you rank your priorities, you can start by deciding which job or project needs your attention before any other. This method will not only ensure that it is done, but also that you do it without enough motivation to do it correctly. Similar to what was said earlier in this book about taking the toughest jobs first, the sooner you start one with a deadline, the more likely you are to complete it on time.

Establishing and ranking your priorities is not a difficult or time-consuming task. If you start each workday with a brief summary of everything you need to accomplish, you can assign top priority to the tasks that must be completed first. Your entire workday will be much smoother, and you will be able to do more.

Maximize your communication skills

Whether you are self-employed or in a busy office, good communication skills should be a standard part of your daily work life. The better you become these skills, the more you will be able to do. In turn, everyone you work with can be more productive.

Some people need to be reminded that good communication skills include knowing the difference between successful communication and wasted time. You may have someone in your office who likes to "visit" coworkers all day long, or always seems to be on the phone. This type of social activity is not appropriate for the workplace. It prevents work from being done.

Good communication skills in the workplace can be summed up in two categories. There is the type of communication that should be as direct, brief and direct as possible. You can say whatever needs to be said, or ask a question, or clarify something, without wasting your own time or the other person's time. The other type of communication is that which involves giving, receiving or exchanging information. You may have to inform someone about an aspect of the work or ask for a detailed explanation about a project. In most cases, these are the only forms of communication that improve the workplace and increase productivity.

Good communication skills also involve being receptive and listening to what the other person is saying. Simply waiting your turn to speak is a negative habit that should have been eliminated in childhood. If you have not yet developed the habit of listening well, it may be helpful to practice this habit during your free time. If you occasionally have lunch or rest with your co-workers, this can be an excellent time to develop your listening skills.

Practicing good communication skills in the workplace saves time. When questions, answers and explanations are received in full when first pronounced, the need for repetition is eliminated. It also gives the other person the message that what they are saying is valuable. When everyone is "on the same path," everyone will do more.

Conclusion: The cornerstone of all success... The strategies!

When you hear the word "productivity," the first thing that comes to mind is probably your job and workplace. The good news is that all of these strategies for increasing productivity are also appropriate for other "places" in life. They are equally useful for students who want to do more with their work in college or high school, and even for housewives who never seem to have enough time to do everything that needs to be done.

There are only twenty-four hours in a day. This is a fact that is equally true for everyone. In the interest of your overall health and well-being, some of those hours should be spent on sleep, recreational activities, and other important health-related habits. Although this still leaves a few hours in the day to do things, your time can be misdirected or wasted if you allow it, or if you're not sure how best to handle those hours.

Get things done strategies focus on how best to manage your work hours for optimal productivity. When you learn not to waste time and make the most of every hour and every day, you'll do more. Instead of feeling stressed, overworked and overloaded, which can lead to less than satisfactory results, the results you get will be real achievements.

Developing and practicing these getting things done strategies won't take much time or effort on your part. Some motivation, and the willingness to start putting it into practice, is really all that is needed. Not only will you see yourself becoming more productive, but you will be able to remember each day as one of your best days.

Now yes, I wish you the best in your results, and remember, everything is practical; theory without action is of no use to you. It brings into real life everything you learn.

A big hug, your friend, Jorge!